CW01262988

WHO FREED THE SLAVES?

History 4th Grade Children's American Civil War Era History Books

BABY PROFESSOR
EDUCATION KIDS

Speedy Publishing LLC
40 E. Main St. #1156
Newark, DE 19711
www.speedypublishing.com
Copyright 2017

All Rights reserved. No part of this book may be reproduced or used in any way or form or by any means whether electronic or mechanical, this means that you cannot record or photocopy any material ideas or tips that are provided in this book.

The first slaves arrived in 1619 in Jamestown, Virginia on a Dutch ship. During the following 200 years, approximately 600,000 more arrived to the colonies in America, mostly to work in the cotton and tobacco fields. In this book, you will read about who freed the slaves and the process that provided them their freedom.

WHERE DID THEY ARRIVE FROM?

They arrived from Africa, mostly from Africa's west coast which were the main ports for the slave trade. The conditions of the ships they traveled on were horrible and they often were packed in the ship's hold, chained and not able to move. Many slaves passed away because of starvation and disease on the ships.

Africa

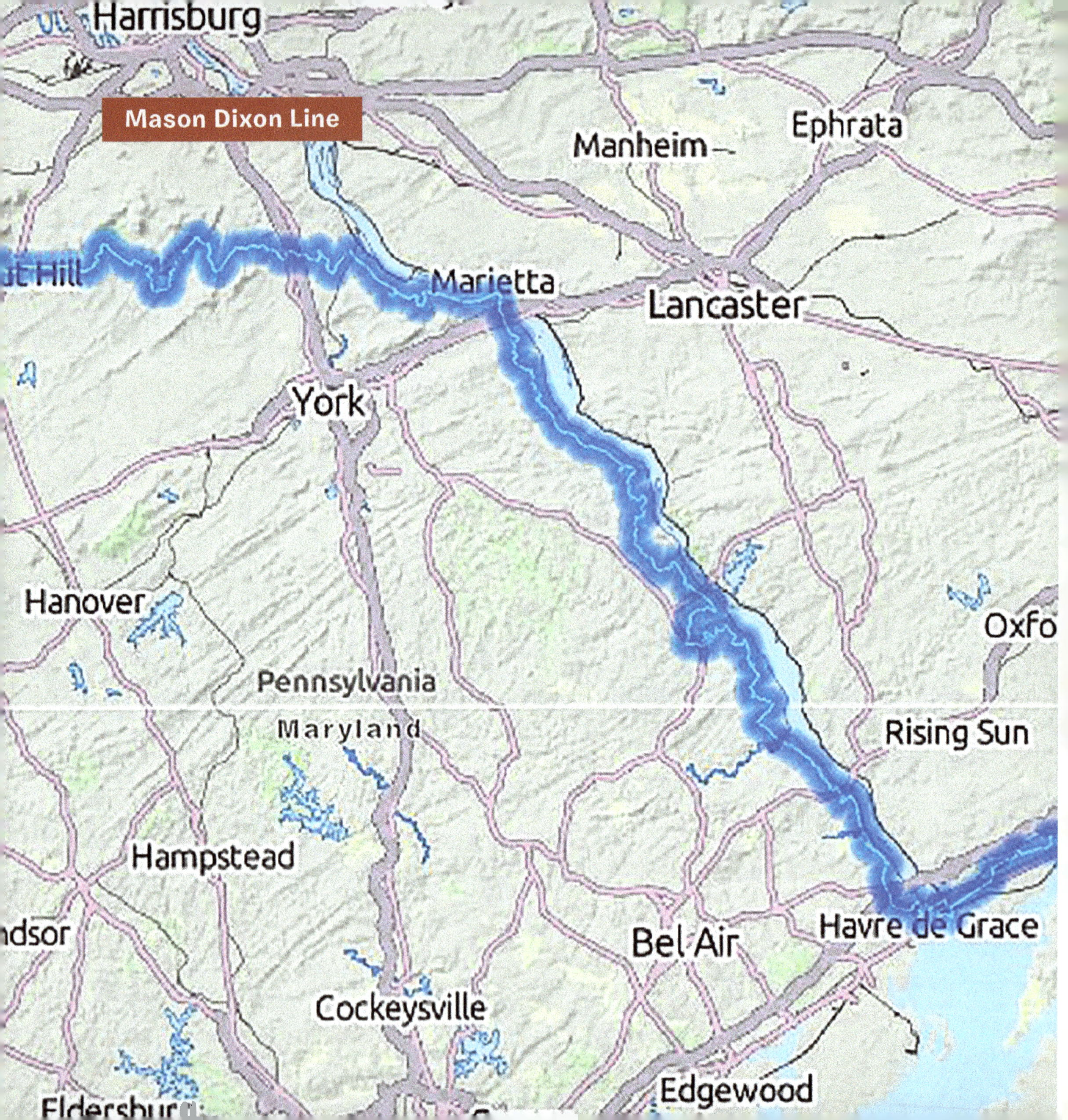
Harrisburg
Mason Dixon Line
Ephrata
Manheim
Marietta
Lancaster
York
Hanover
Oxfo
Pennsylvania
Maryland
Rising Sun
Hampstead
ndsor
Havre de Grace
Bel Air
Cockeysville
Edgewood

ABOLITIONISM

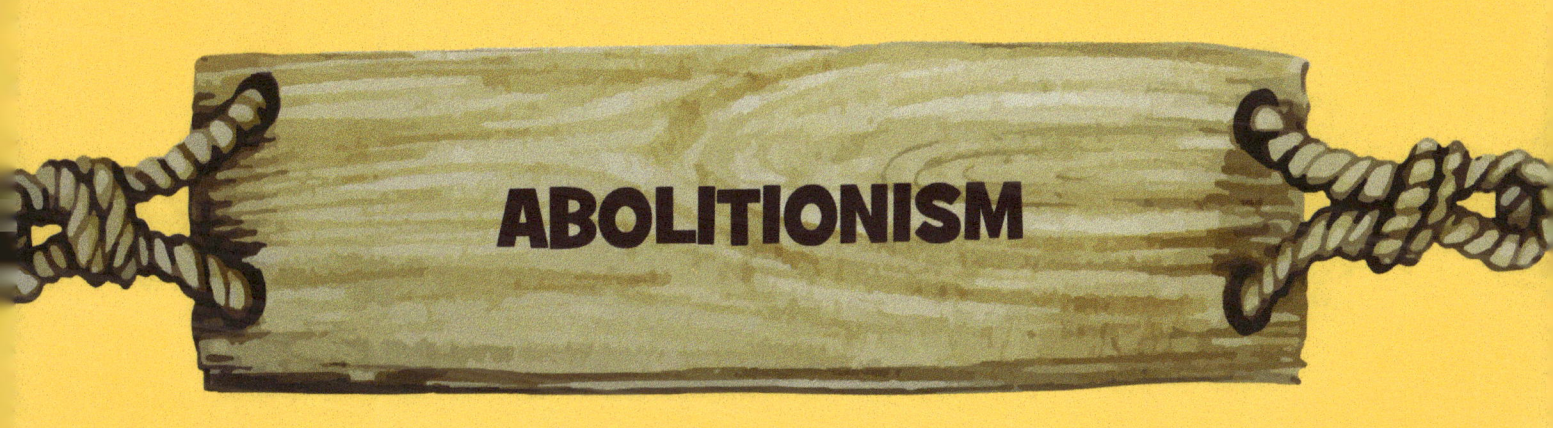

Many of the northern states had outlawed slavery after the revolution. Most slaves living north of the Mason Dixon Line were let go and set free by 1840. Most people living in the north believed that it should be illegal in all of the States. They became known as abolitionists since their desire was to abolish slavery.

UNDERGROUND RAILROAD

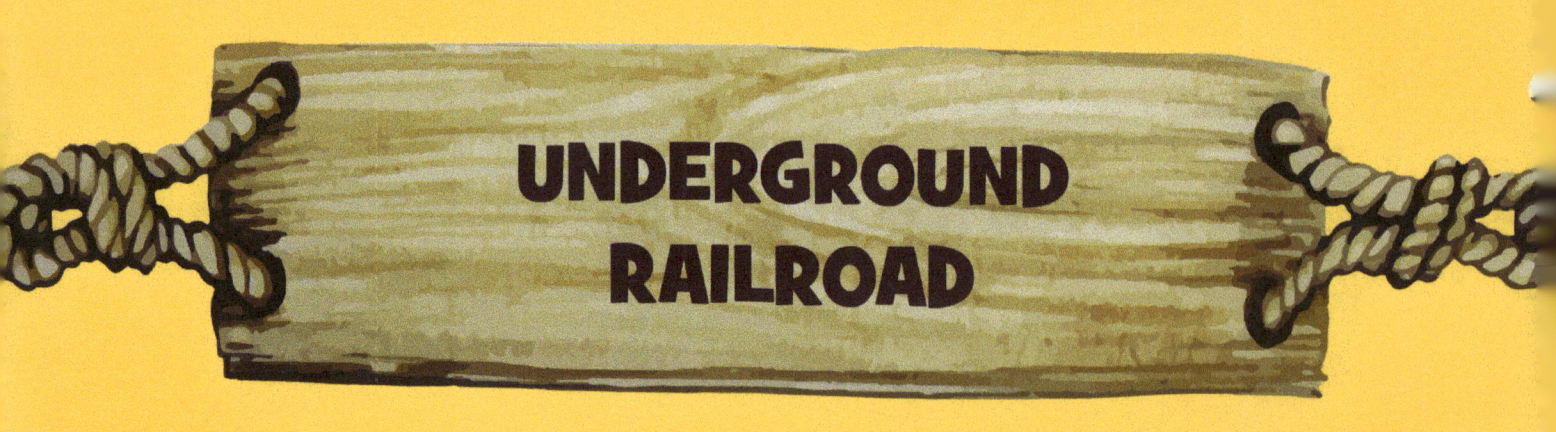

The Underground Railroad was a way for slaves in the south to escape to the north. The Railroad consisted of many homes, hideouts, and people helping the slaves to go north in secret. Between 1810 and 1865, about 100,000 slaves successfully escaped this way.

Underground Railroad

Civil War

CIVIL WAR

Once Lincoln became president, the south feared that he would make slavery illegal. This is how the Civil War began. However, the war was won by the North and the states in the south again joined the Union.

THE EMANCIPATION PROCLAMATION

The Emancipation Proclamation was issued on January 1, 1863, by President Lincoln as an executive order and presidential proclamation. It was issued to amend the federal status of over 3 million slaves in certain areas of the South from being a "slave" to being "free", however, its original effect was less than desired.

By the President of the United States of America.

Whereas, On the Twenty-Second day of September, in the year of our Lord one thousand eight hundred and sixty-two, a Proclamation was issued by the President of the United States, containing, among other things the following, to wit:

"That on the first day of January, in the year of our Lord one thousand eight hundred and sixty-three, all persons held as Slaves within any State or designated part of a State, the people whereof shall then be in rebellion against the United States, shall be then, thenceforth, and **FOREVER FREE,** and the EXECUTIVE GOVERNMENT OF THE UNITED STATES, including the military and naval authorities thereof, WILL RECOGNIZE AND MAINTAIN THE FREEDOM of such persons, and will do no act or acts to repress such persons, or any of them, in any efforts they may make for their actual freedom.

"That the Executive will, on the first day of January aforesaid, by proclamation, designate the States and parts of States, if any, in which the people thereof respectively shall then be in rebellion against the United States, and the fact that any State, or the people thereof shall on that day be in good faith represented in the Congress of the United States by members chosen thereto at elections wherein a majority of the qualified voters of such State shall have participated, shall, in the absence of strong countervailing testimony be deemed conclusive evidence that such State and the people thereof are not then in rebellion against the United States."

Now, therefore, I, ABRAHAM LINCOLN, PRESIDENT OF THE UNITED STATES, by virtue of the power in me vested as **Commander-in-Chief of the Army and Navy** of the United States in time of actual armed Rebellion against the authority and government of the United States, and as a fit and necessary war measure for suppressing said Rebellion, do, on this first day of January, in the year of our Lord one thousand eight hundred and sixty-three, and in accordance with my purpose so to do, publicly proclaim for the full period of one hundred days from the day of the first above-mentioned order, and designate, as the States and parts of States wherein the people thereof respectively are this day in rebellion against the United States, the following, to wit: ARKANSAS, TEXAS, LOUISIANA (except the Parishes of St. Bernard, Plaquemines, Jefferson, St. John, St. Charles, St. James, Ascension, Assumption, Terre Bonne, La Fourche, St. Mary, St. Martin, and Orleans, including the City of Orleans), MISSISSIPPI, ALABAMA, FLORIDA, GEORGIA, SOUTH CAROLINA, NORTH CAROLINA, AND VIRGINIA (except the forty-eight counties designated as West Virginia, and also the counties of Berkeley, Accomac, Northampton, Elizabeth City, York, Princess Ann, and Norfolk, including the cities of Norfolk and Portsmouth), and which excepted parts are for the present left precisely as if this Proclamation were not issued.

And by virtue of the power and for the purpose aforesaid, I do order and declare that **ALL PERSONS HELD AS SLAVES** within said designated States and parts of States ARE, AND HENCEFORWARD **SHALL BE FREE!** and that the Executive Government of the United States, including the Military and Naval Authorities thereof, will RECOGNIZE AND MAINTAIN THE FREEDOM of said persons.

And I hereby enjoin upon the people so declared to be free, to abstain from all violence, UNLESS IN NECESSARY SELF-DEFENCE, and I recommend to them that in all cases, when allowed, they LABOR FAITHFULLY FOR REASONABLE WAGES.

And I further declare and make known that such persons of suitable condition will be received into the armed service of the United States, to garrison forts, positions, stations, and other places, and to man vessels of all sorts in said service.

And upon this act, SINCERELY BELIEVED TO BE AN ACT OF JUSTICE, warranted by the Constitution, upon military necessity, I invoke the considerate judgment of mankind, and the gracious favor of ALMIGHTY GOD.

In testimony whereof I have hereunto set my name, and caused the seal of the United States to be affixed.

[L. S.] Done at the CITY OF WASHINGTON, this first day of January, in the year of our Lord one thousand eight hundred and sixty-three, and of the Independence of the United States the eighty-seventh.

A. Lincoln

By the President.

William H. Seward

Secretary of State.

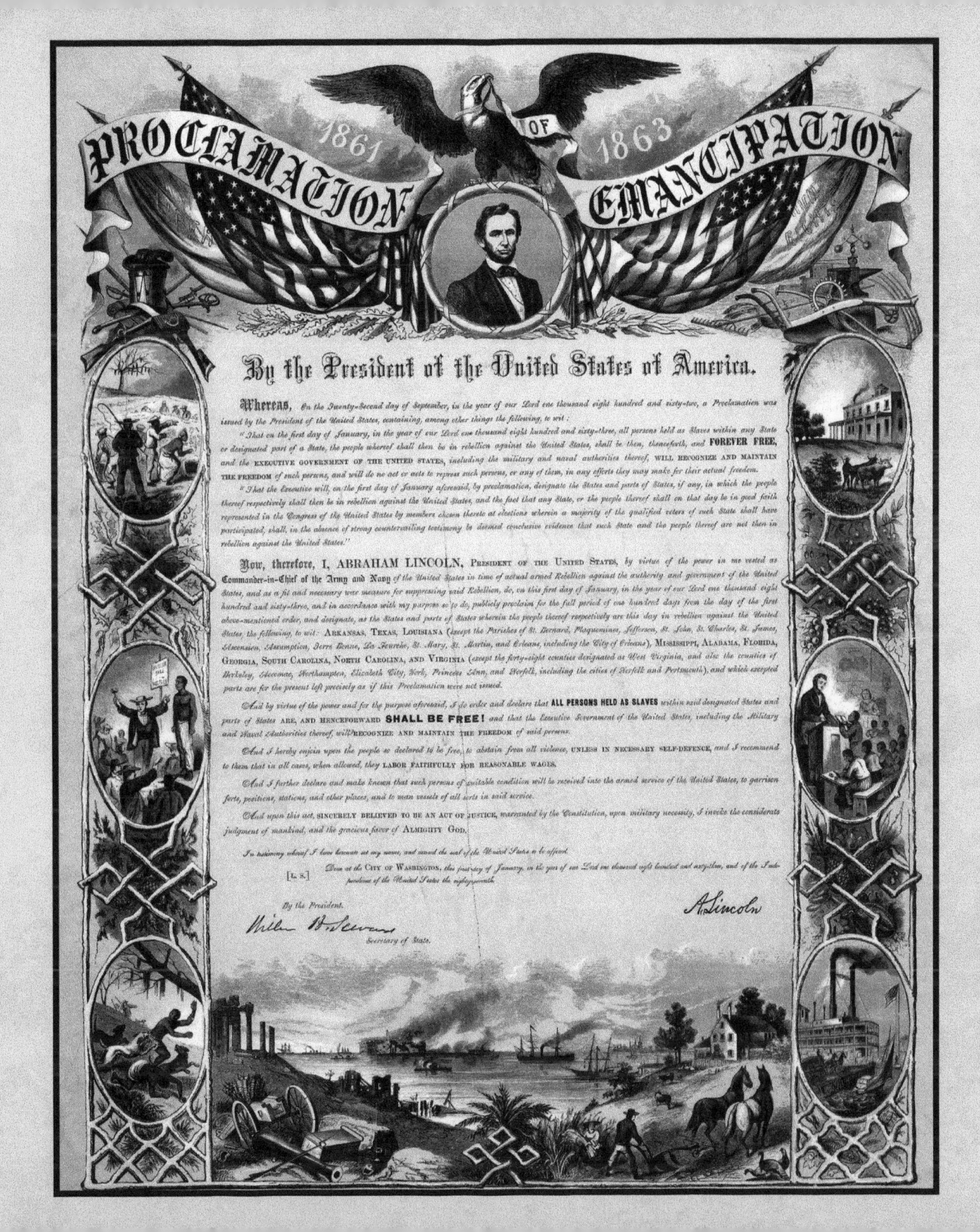

First Reading of the Emancipation Proclamation

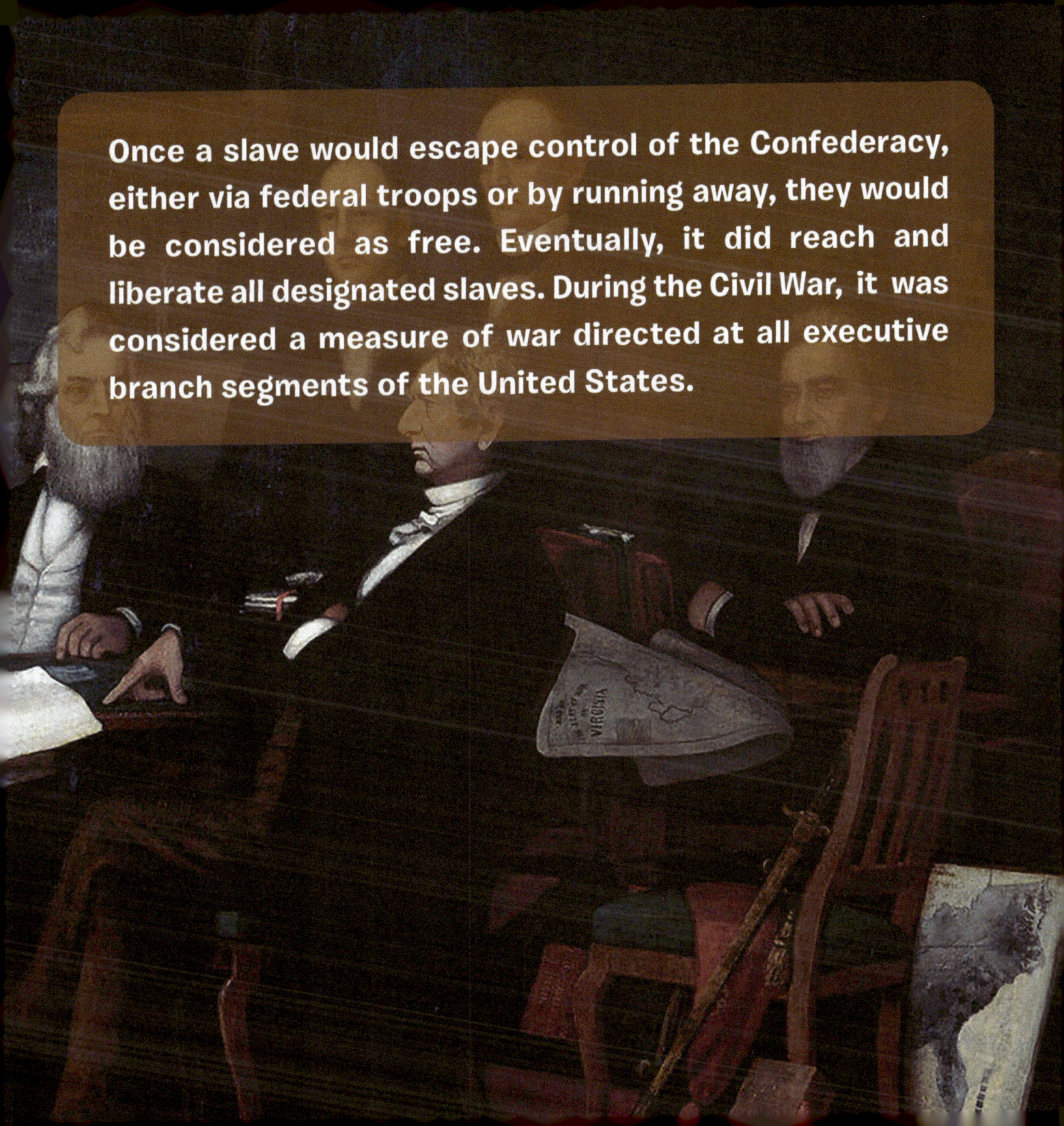

Once a slave would escape control of the Confederacy, either via federal troops or by running away, they would be considered as free. Eventually, it did reach and liberate all designated slaves. During the Civil War, it was considered a measure of war directed at all executive branch segments of the United States.

The original Emancipation Proclamation document consisted of five pages and is currently stored in Washington, D.C. at the National Archives.

National Archives Building

Abraham Lincoln

GOVERNMENTAL ACTION TOWARDS EMANCIPATION

Lincoln first sent his annual message to Congress in December of 1861. During this message, he commended the free labor system and endorsed legislation addressing the status of contraband slaves as well as slaves located in the loyal states, either by way of buying freedom with federal taxes, or with funds and efforts of voluntary colonization.

Thaddeus Stevens, in 1862, who was the Republican Leader of the House, called for war against this rebellion to include emancipation of the slaves, argued that emancipation, would ruin the rebel economy.

Thaddeus Stevens

Emancipation Day

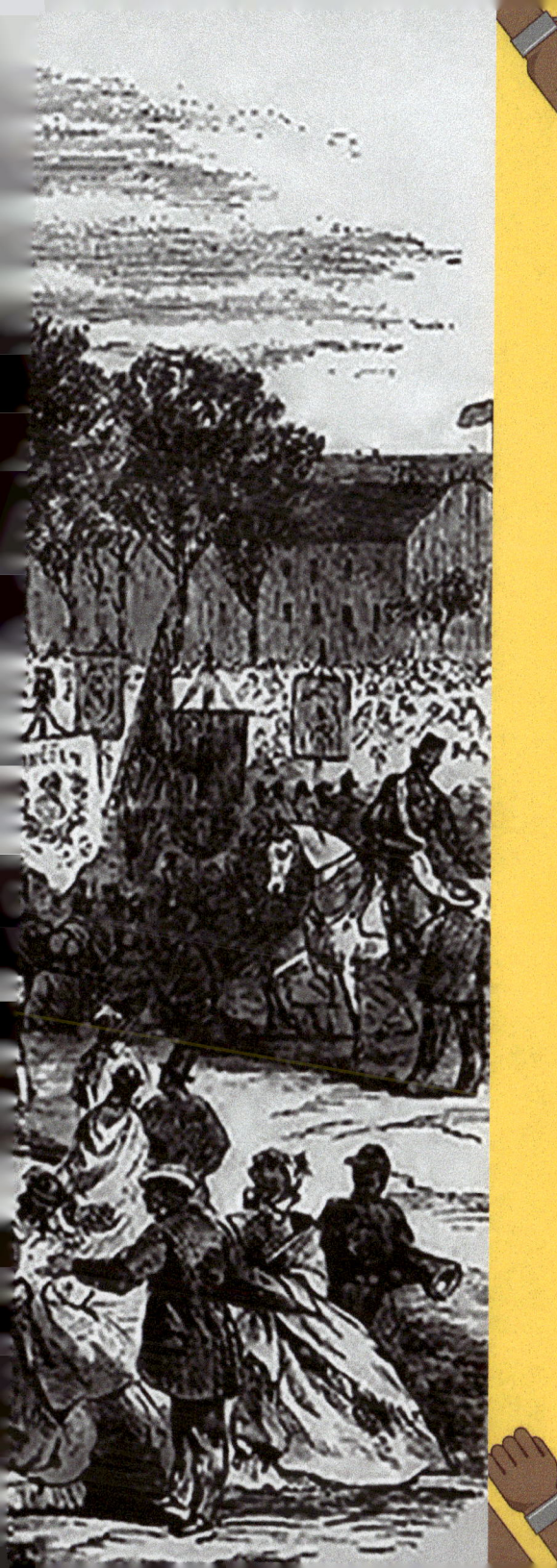

Congress, on March 13, 1862, approved a "Law Enacting an Additional Article of War", stating that from now on it would be forbidden for the Union Army to return any fugitive slaves to their original owner. On April 10, 1862, Congress then announced that the government would provide compensation to the owners of the slaves who would set their slaves free. On April 16, 1862, the District of Columbia freed their slaves, and the owners were then compensated.

Congress then proceeded to prohibit slavery for all current and future territories of the United States on June 19, 1862, and the President quickly signed this piece of legislation. This act reputed the 1857 opinion of the United States Supreme Court in the case of Dred Scott stating that Congress had no power to regulate slavery in the territories of the United States.

The Old Supreme Court Chamber in the Capitol

Thomas Jefferson

This action by President Lincoln and Congress also shut down the idea of popular sovereignty which was advanced by Stephen A. Douglas to be an answer to this controversy, as well as completing the first legislative effort proposed by Thomas Jefferson in 1784, confining slavery to remain within the existing states.

Congress then passed and President Lincoln signed the Confiscation Act of 1862 in July, which contained provisions that court proceedings liberating slaves be held by "rebels" that had been convicted, or by slaves of rebels which had escaped. This Act applied to cases of criminal convictions and those that had been slaves to "disloyal" masters.

President Abraham Lincoln

Abraham Lincoln

Lincoln's position, however, continued to state that Congress did not have the power to free all slaves within borders of states held by rebels, but as commander in chief, Lincoln had the power to do this if he felt it was proper military measure, and he had already drafted the plans for this action.

WERE THEY ALL SET FREE RIGHT AWAY?

Of the 4 million slaves, only approximately 50,000 were set free immediately. The Proclamation had its limitations. First, only the slaves that were in Confederate States not under Union control were set free. Some border states and certain areas were not set free immediately. For the remaining states in the South, they would be set free until the Union was able to win over the Confederacy.

Slaves and Rebel Officers

Union Army

However, it eventually did set free millions of slaves.

It also made it possible for Black men to be soldiers for the Union Army. Approximately 200,000 black soldiers fought for the Union Army helping for the North to win as well as helping to expand the freedom areas when they would march through the South.

BORDER STATES

During the Civil War, the slave states that did not want to leave the Union were known as the border states. These states consisted of Missouri, Maryland, Kentucky, and Delaware. West Virginia, after separating from Virginia, was also referred to as a border state.

Civil War

Abraham Lincoln

WHY DID PRESIDENT LINCOLN WAIT UNTIL 1863?

He wanted to have a major victory so as to have full support behind the Proclamation. If he did not have public support when he issued it, it may have failed. Lincoln wanted to make sure it was successful and considered a great victory for the North.

Once the Union turned back General Lee and the Confederates on September 17, 1862 at the Battle of Antietam, he knew this was the time. The original announcement that the order was coming was provided within a few days on September 22, 1862.

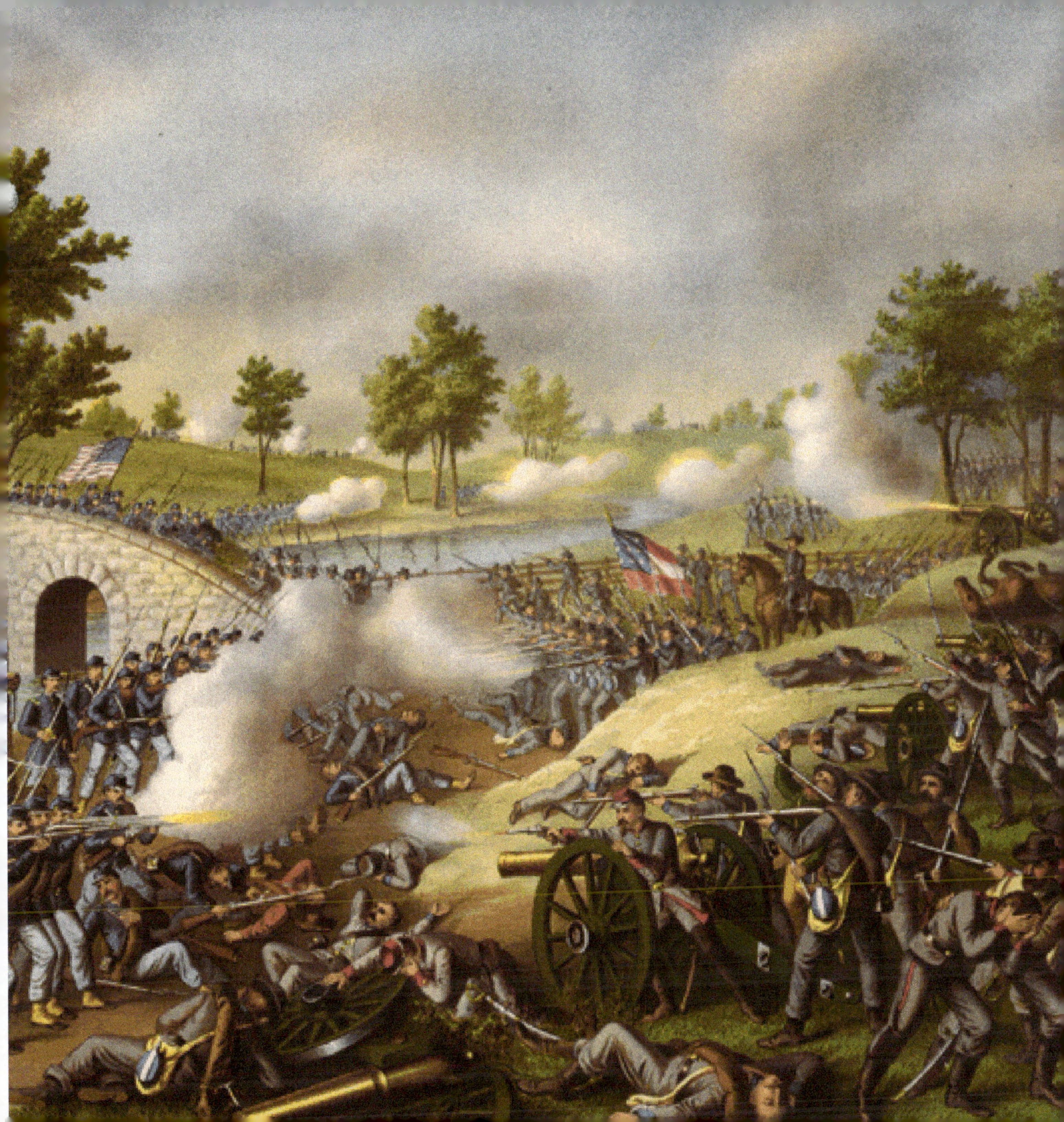

General Robert E. Lee

GENERAL ROBERT E. LEE

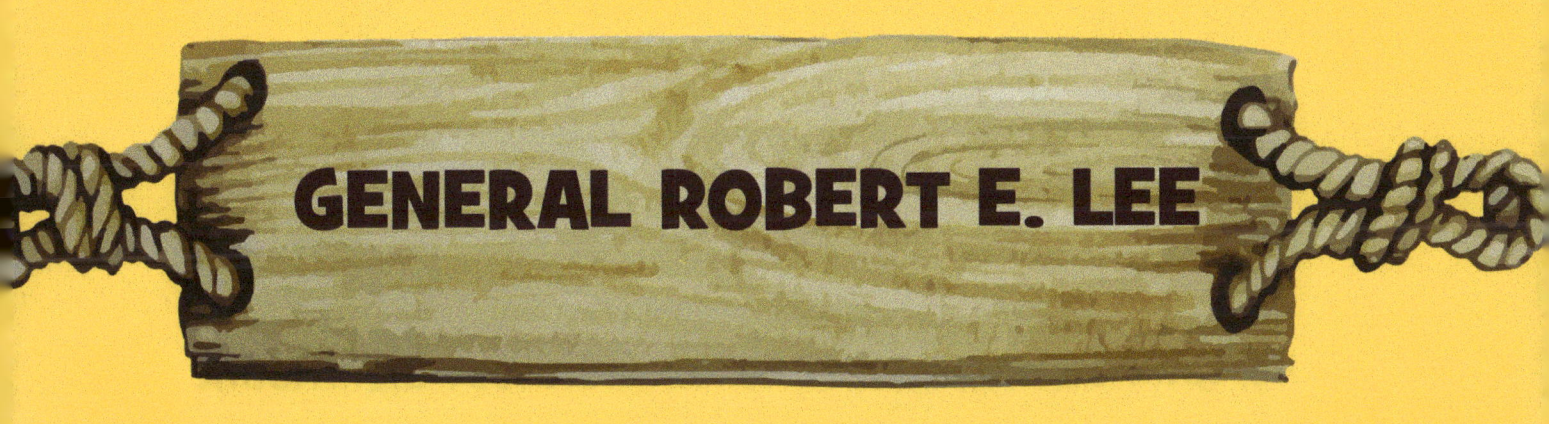

In 1861, at the beginning of the Civil War, General Lee was offered to command the Union Army by Lincoln. However, Lee was loyal to Virginia, his home state. While he did not like slavery, he believed that he could not fight against Virginia. He proceeded to leave the United States Army and then became the General for the Confederate Army of Virginia.

He took command of one of the most significant armies during the War. He selected talented officers including Jeb Stuart and Thomas "Stonewall" Jackson. Even though the Confederate armies were always outnumbered, Lee and his soldiers were able to win several battles with their courage and brilliance.

Meeting of Robert E. Lee and Stonewall Jackson

General Robert E. Lee surrenders at Appomattox Court House

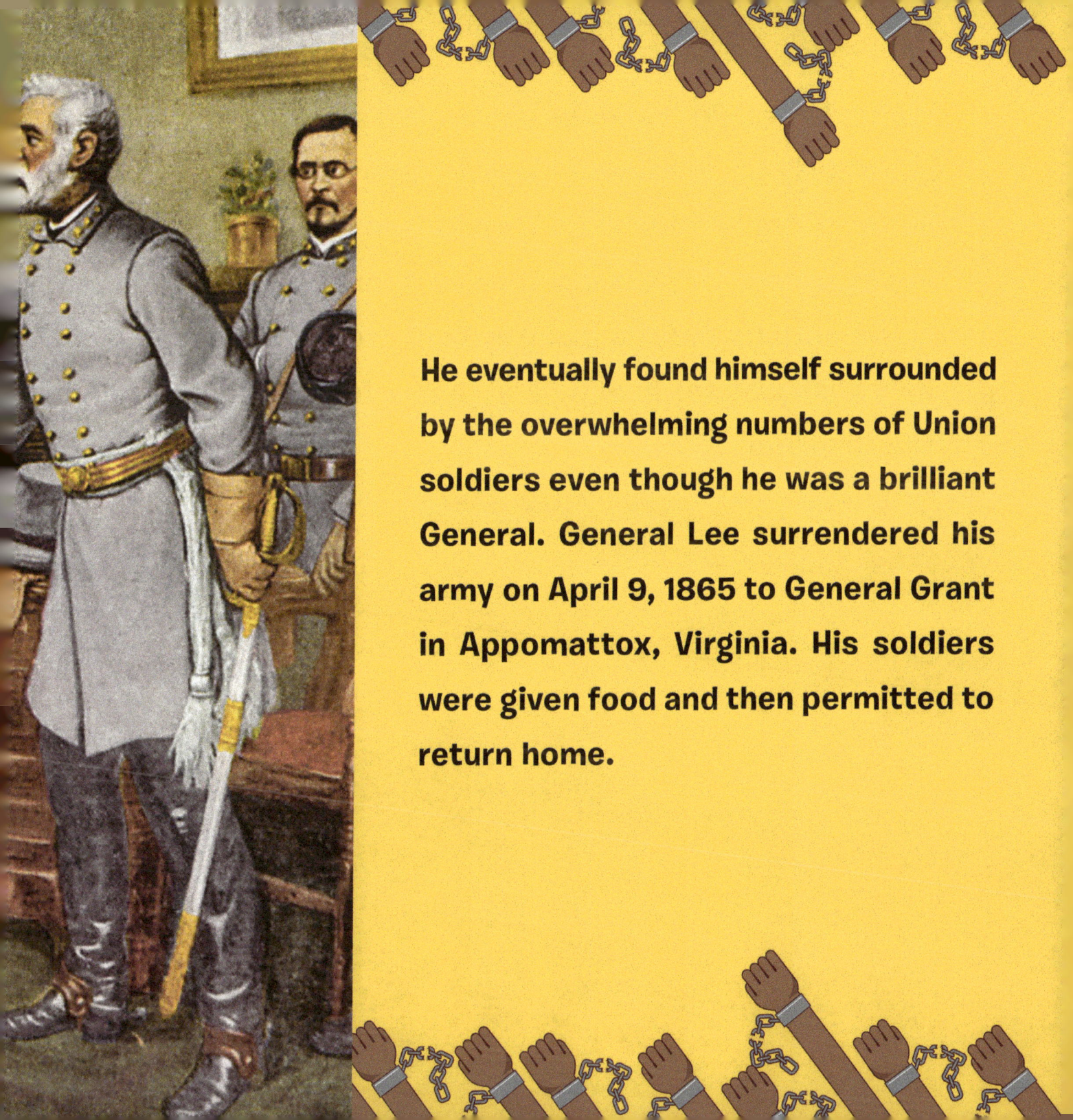

He eventually found himself surrounded by the overwhelming numbers of Union soldiers even though he was a brilliant General. General Lee surrendered his army on April 9, 1865 to General Grant in Appomattox, Virginia. His soldiers were given food and then permitted to return home.

While he could have been tried as a traitor and possibly hung, President Lincoln forgave him. Lee then became the president of Washington College located in Lexington, Virginia. He worked there as long as he could until he passed away in 1870 from a stroke. His only wish was for healing and peace for the U.S. after the Civil War.

Washington College

Emancipation Proclamation

THE THIRTEENTH AMENDMENT

Since the Emancipation Proclamation was issued as an executive order, it was not yet Constitutional law. It did, however, create the path for the Thirteenth Amendment. The Proclamation's advantage was it would be able to happen sooner. The Thirteenth Amendment then took a few additional years for passage by congress and implementation, but was adopted on December 6, 1865, becoming part of our U.S. Constitution.

The Thirteenth Amendment reads as follows:

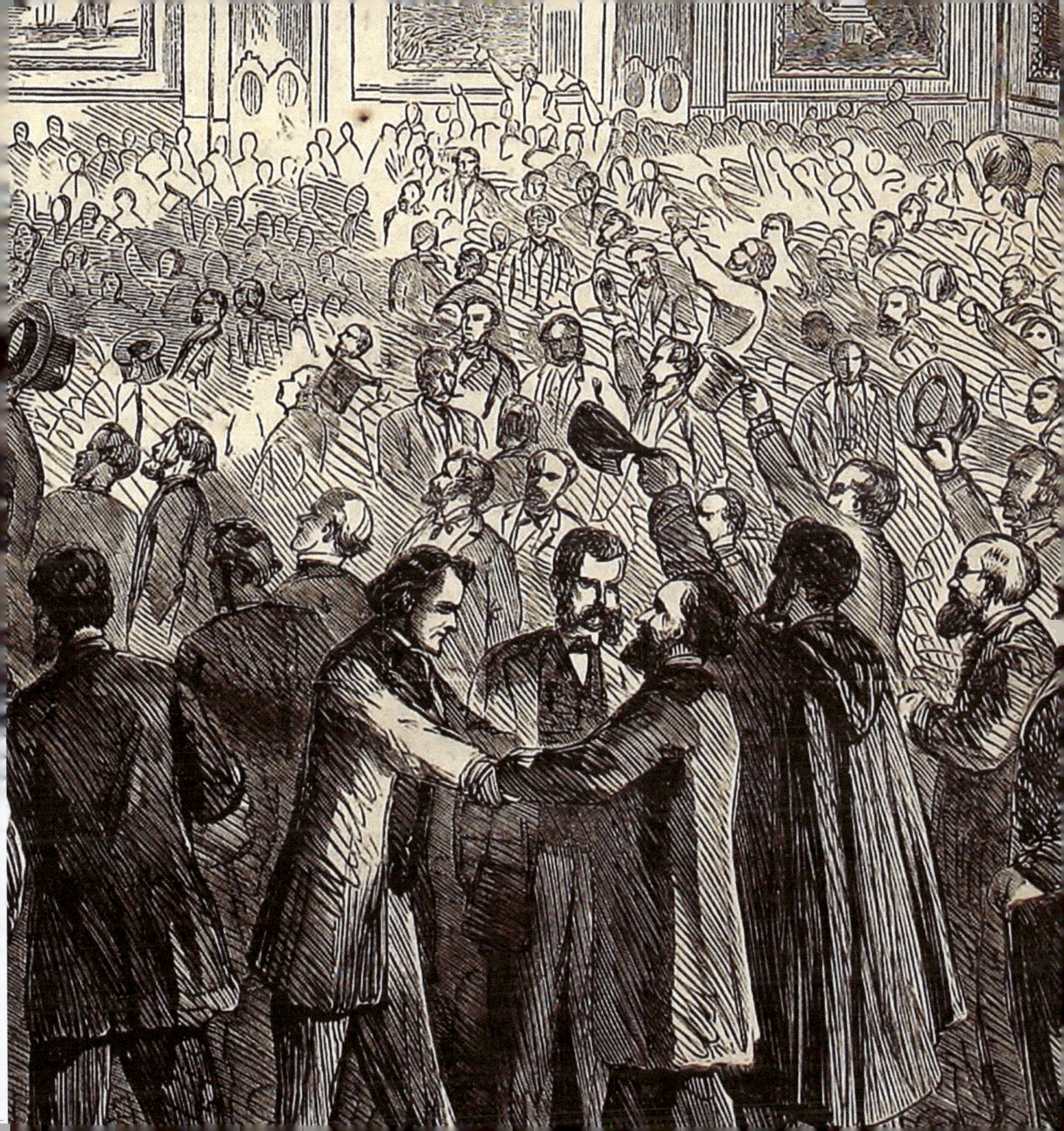

Slaves working on a plantation

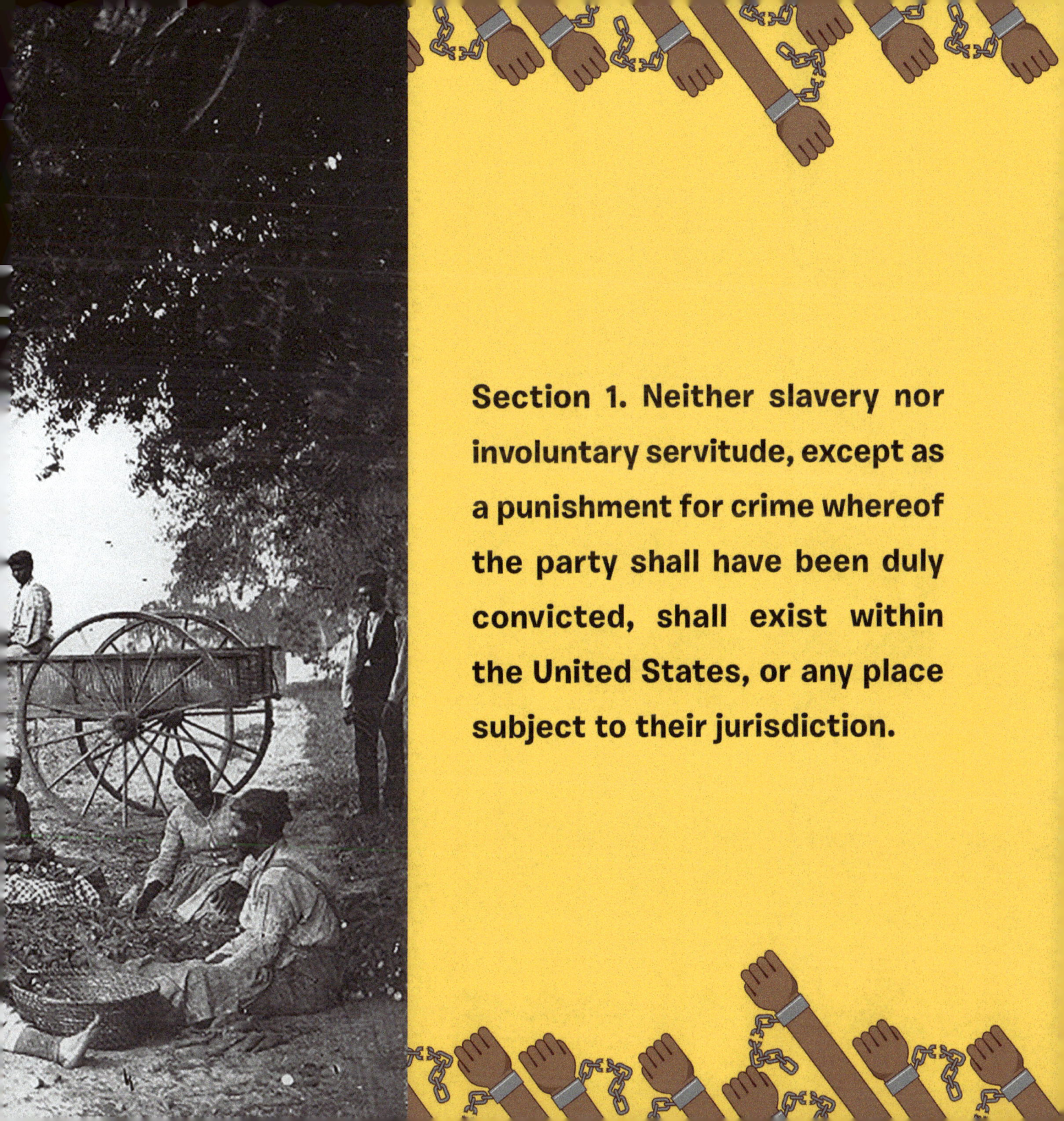

Section 1. Neither slavery nor involuntary servitude, except as a punishment for crime whereof the party shall have been duly convicted, shall exist within the United States, or any place subject to their jurisdiction.

Section 2. Congress shall have power to enforce this article by appropriate legislation.

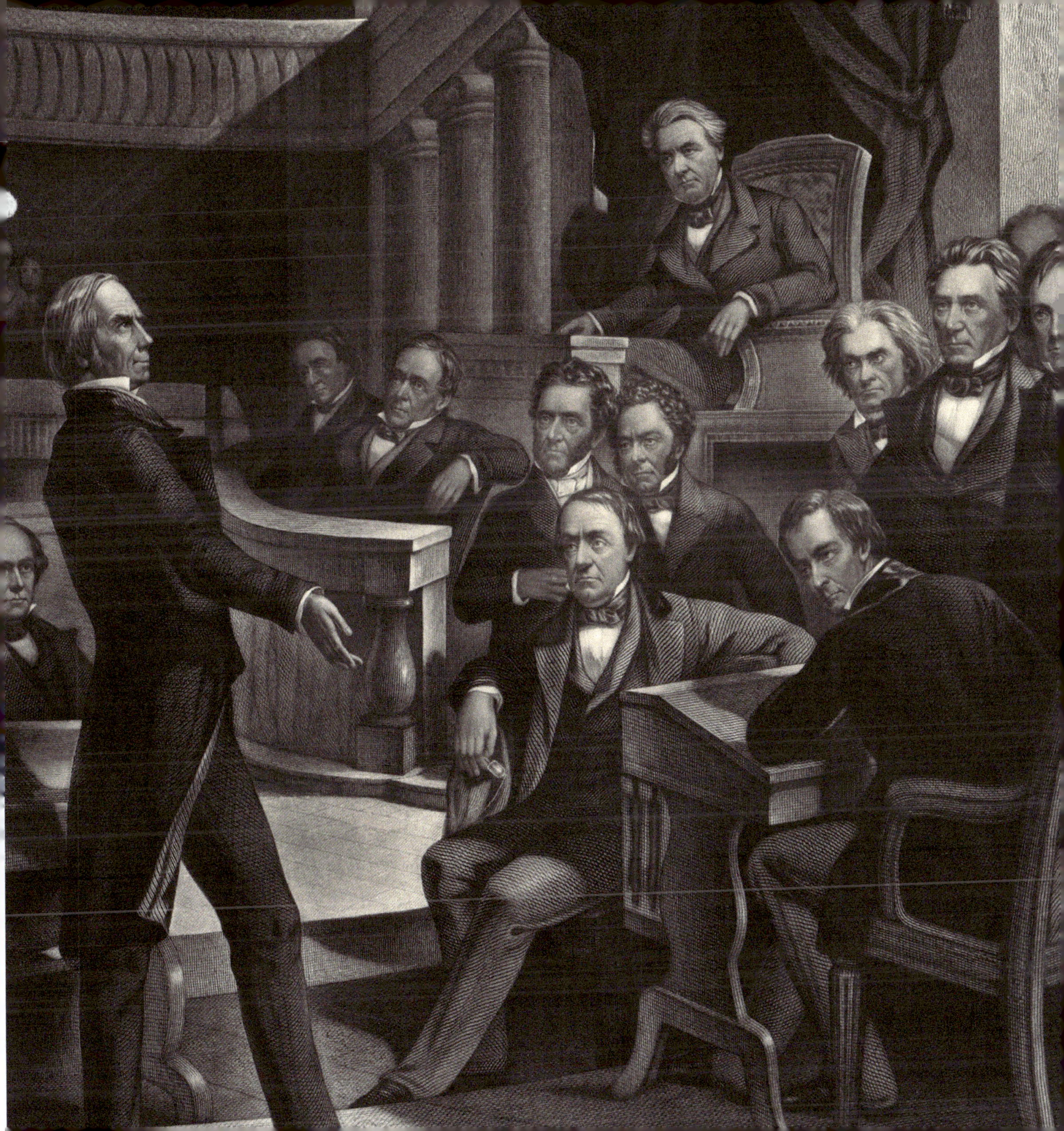

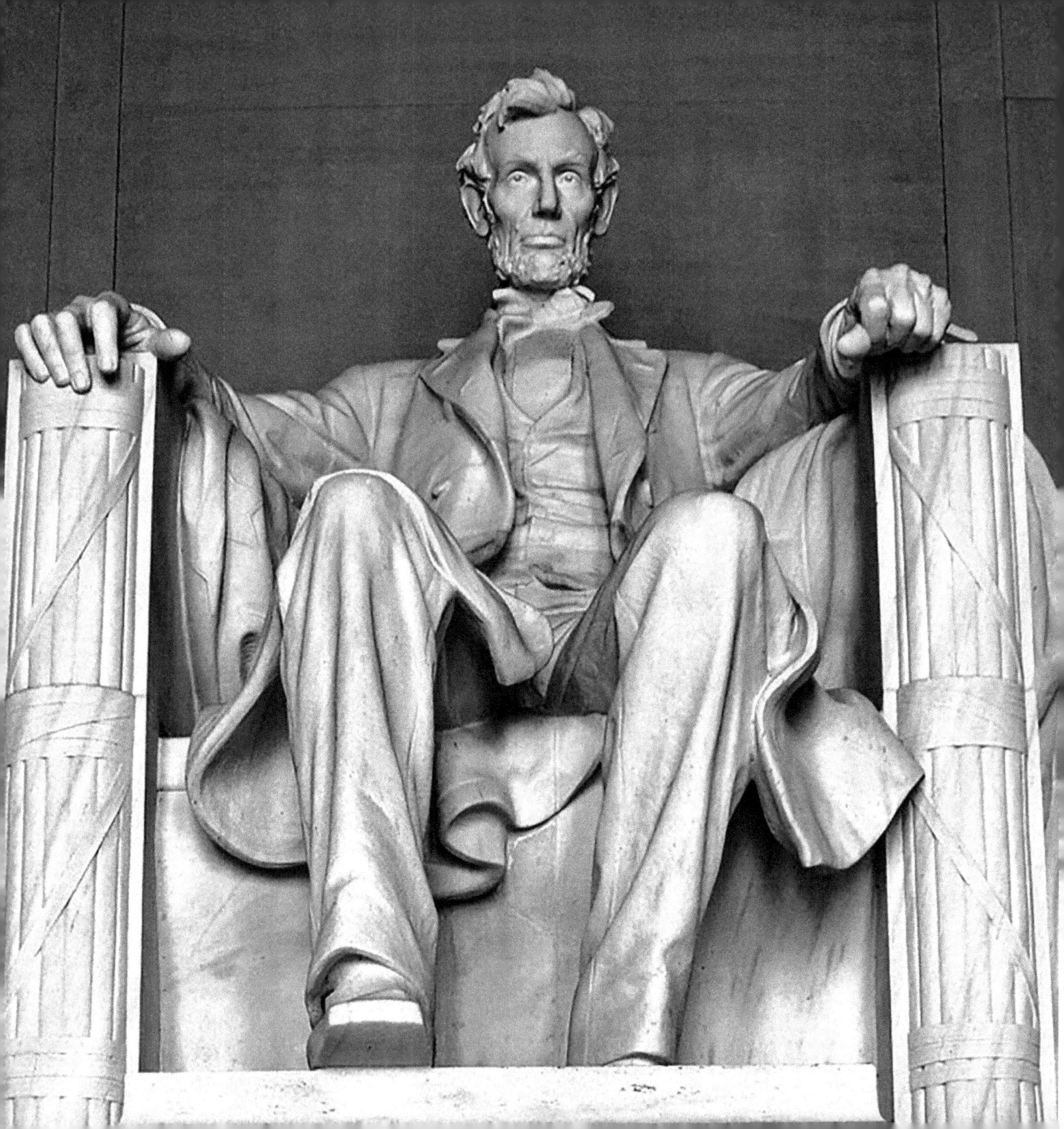

THE GETTYSBURG ADDRESS

In his Gettysburg Address, Lincoln made an indirect reference to the Emancipation Proclamation and the end to slavery as a goal of the war, using the phrase "new birth of freedom". Lincoln's support of the quickly growing element of abolitionism within the Republican Party was solidified and made sure they would not block his 1864 re-nomination.

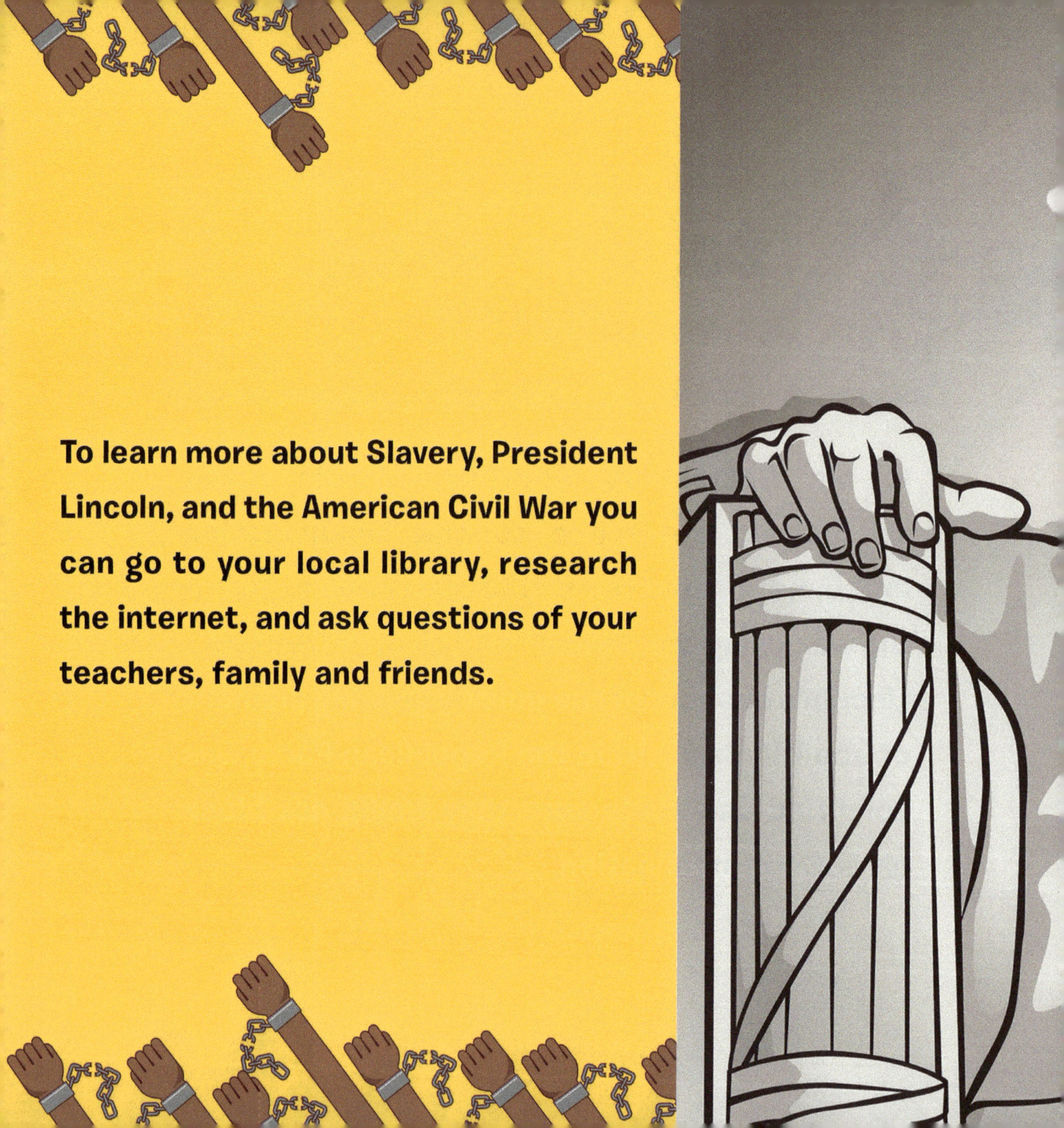

To learn more about Slavery, President Lincoln, and the American Civil War you can go to your local library, research the internet, and ask questions of your teachers, family and friends.

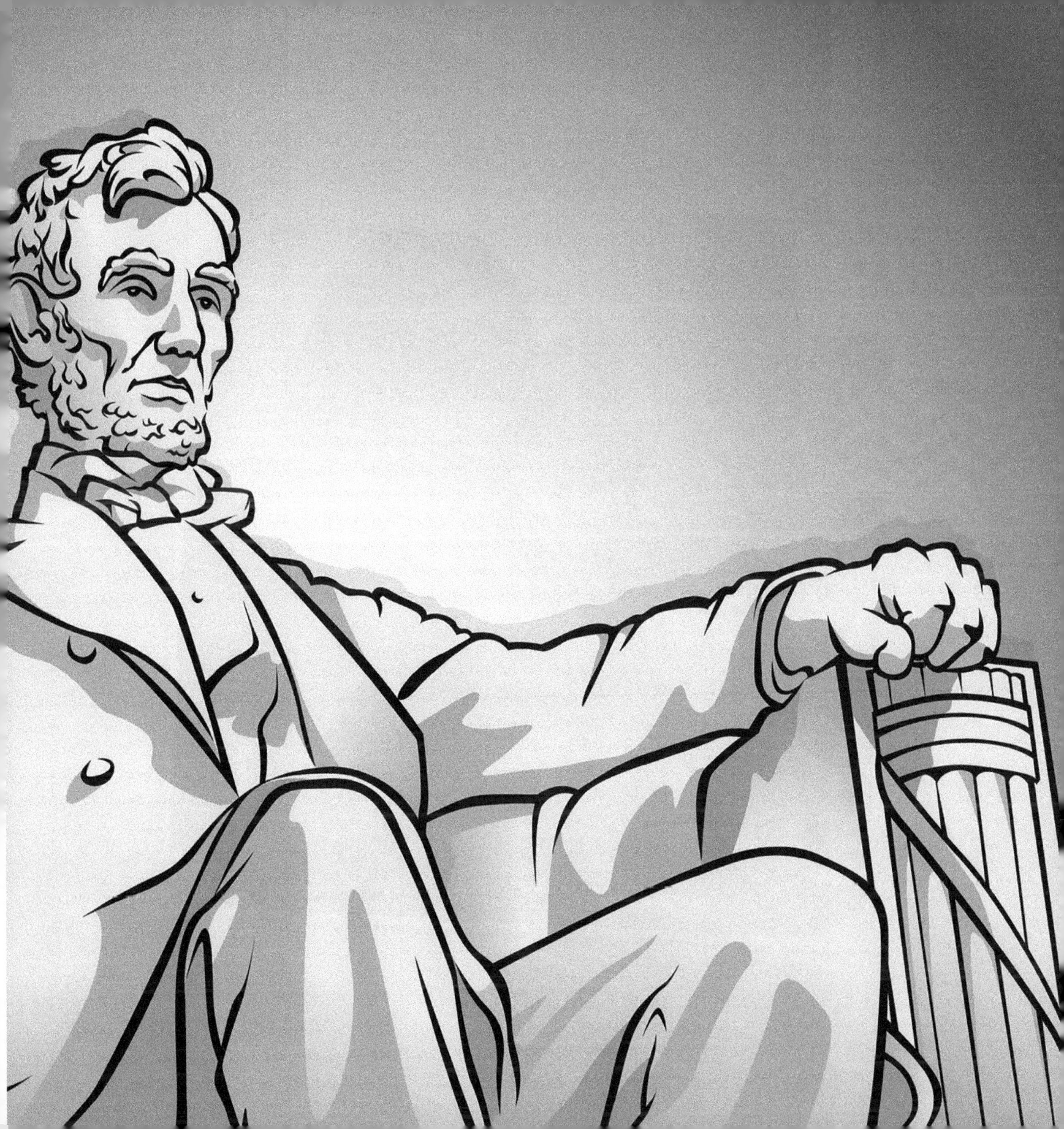

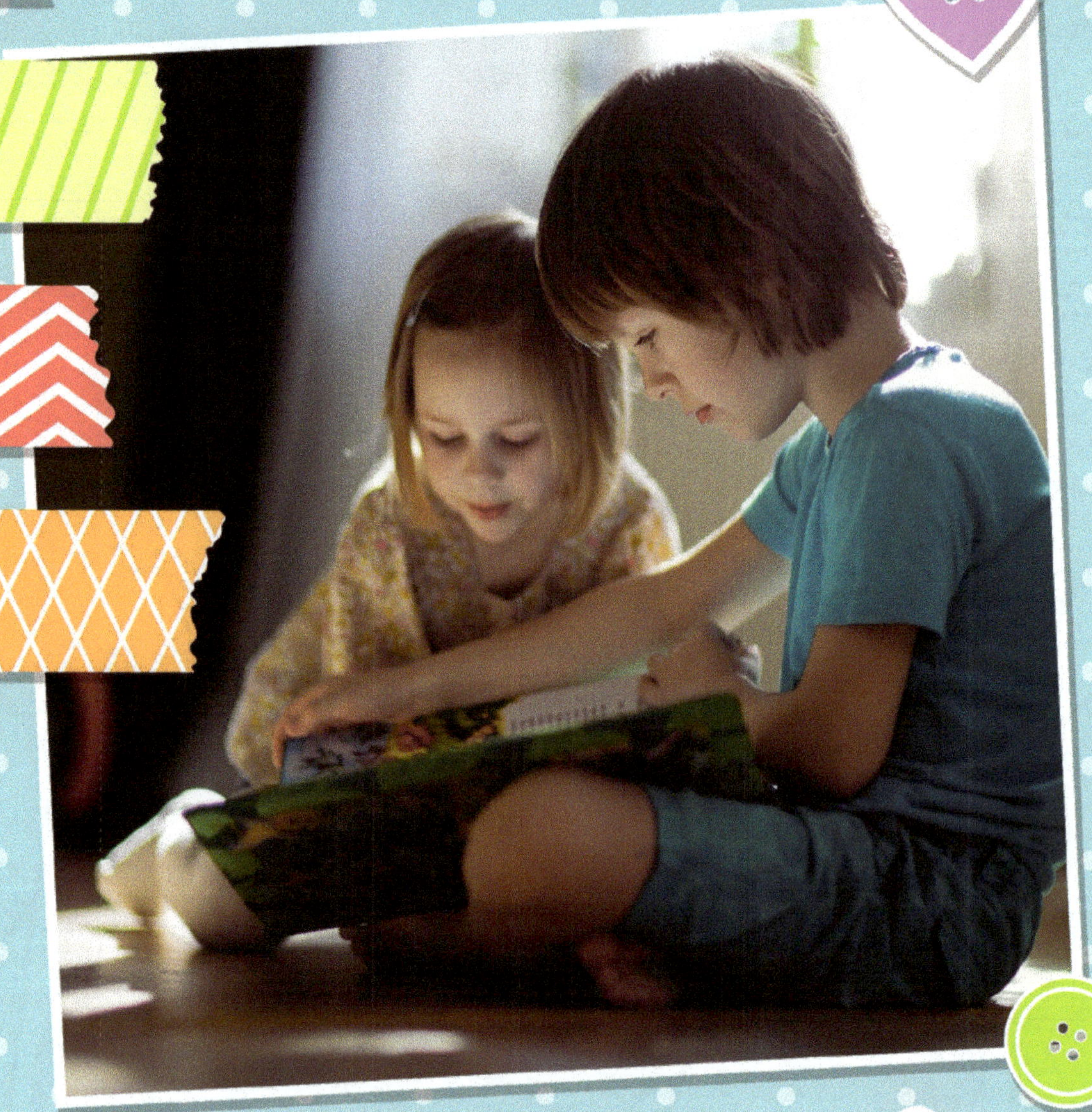

Visit

BABY PROFESSOR
EDUCATION KIDS

www.BabyProfessorBooks.com

to download Free Baby Professor eBooks
and view our catalog of new and exciting
Children's Books

Milton Keynes UK
Ingram Content Group UK Ltd.
UKHW051050070924
447802UK00025B/390

9 798869 417923